LUTHERANS IN THE U.S.A.

Revised Edition

Willmar Thorkelson

AUGSBURG PUBLISHING HOUSE

Minneapolis   **Minnesota**

LUTHERANS IN THE U.S.A.

1978 Revised Edition

Copyright © 1969, 1978 Augsburg Publishing House

Library of Congress Catalog Card No. 77-84812

International Standard Book No. 0-8066-1688-1

MANUFACTURED IN THE UNITED STATES OF AMERICA

Contents

Introduction

MARTIN LUTHER, as nearly everyone knows, never intended to start a new church.

But the Reformation that the German monk began in 1517 swept across the European continent and Scandinavia, and from there was carried across seas and oceans by explorers, colonists, and missionaries.

Today his followers are estimated at 75 million in 80 countries—a third of all Protestants in the world. About half of them are found in East and West Germany. A fourth more are in Scandinavia—Sweden, Denmark, Finland, and Norway—where the state religion is Lutheran.

This leaves the remaining fourth in North America and in the rest of the world. In the United States there are nearly nine million Lutherans, making them the nation's third largest Protestant group after the Baptists and Methodists.

Lutheran immigrants came to America in the early 17th century. The first settlers were Dutch merchants who arrived in New Amsterdam in 1624. A group of Swedish

Lutherans established the colony of New Sweden along the Delaware River in 1638. In the 1730s, the great wave of German immigration to America began. Thousands of German Lutherans swarmed into Pennsylvania and adjoining colonies.

The Revolutionary War slowed down immigration a bit, but by 1800 there were an estimated 40,000 Lutherans in the new nation. Over the years some of the early settlers and constantly arriving immigrants pushed west and south in successive waves of settlement, with each new wave penetrating farther into the wilderness. A group of Saxons from Germany came up the Mississippi River to Missouri in 1839.

The depression that hit northern Europe after the Napoleonic wars and the French Revolution brought the first wave of immigrants to this country from Scandinavia. Many of them traveled halfway across the country and settled in Illinois and Wisconsin and elsewhere in the Mississippi River valley.

The Civil War again slowed arrivals from Europe, but when it was over, there was a new flood of immigrants. The years from 1865 to 1900 brought the vast majority of Germans and Scandinavians to this country.

Lutherans came to this country for a wide variety of reasons. Many hoped to improve their economic lot. Others wanted to escape military service or to find anonymity and adventure. For still others the reasons were religious— to find greater freedom of worship than they had in their homelands.

Wherever they settled, Lutheran immigrants brought with them their Bibles and hymnals in their native languages and the traditions they had learned. Sometimes pastors came with them; sometimes worship was lay-conducted.

Gradually congregations were formed, and later these were grouped together into synods. The congregations and synods often had hyphenated names, reflecting the European origins of their people. There were German-Lutheran churches for the Germans, Swedish-Lutheran for the Swedes, Danish-Lutheran for the Danes, etc.

As the people became more Americanized, they began to use English in their services and the foreign labels were dropped from church names. Lutheran churches reached out and took into their memberships hundreds of thousands of new members who had no trace of German or Scandinavian ancestry.

A high price was paid for the fragmentation that had taken place in American Lutheranism—fragmentation that resulted not only because of differences in language and culture but also because of differences in theological emphasis and in practice. Lutherans found themselves set apart from other Lutherans in dozens of competing synods.

Eventually Lutheran synods started to draw together in cooperative councils and in organic unions. The need to minister together to Lutheran servicemen in World War I resulted in formation of the predecessor agency of the National Lutheran Council, which performed heroic service in relief and rehabilitation during and after World War II. Later, when mergers reduced the bodies in the council to two, a new cooperative agency bringing in two more Lutheran bodies was formed. It was the Lutheran Council in the U.S.A. On the international level the Lutheran World Federation became the cooperative agency of churches with about three-fourths of the world's Lutherans.

The many organic unions that took place in the late 19th century and in this century brought almost 95% of the nine million Lutherans of North America into three large bodies. The other 5% are divided among 10 bodies.

Succeeding chapters describe how these Lutheran church bodies came into existence and their distinctive characteristics. Needless to say, this small book is not a complete history of U.S. Lutheranism. It is rather a journalist's report of some of the major developments, especially those of recent years.

The Lutheran Church in America

THE Lutheran Church in America is the largest, most Americanized, most urban, most ecumenical, and most socially conscious of the Lutheran bodies of North America.

It was organized only in 1962, but its American roots go back to the 17th century Dutch-speaking Lutheran churches in New Netherland (now New York), the 17th century Swedish-speaking Lutheran churches on the Delaware River, and the 18th century German-speaking Lutheran churches of Pennsylvania, New York, New Jersey, Maryland, Virginia, the Carolinas, Georgia, and Nova Scotia.

Today it spans the United States and Canada with more than three million members in some 6000 congregations and 33 synods.

The LCA bears the imprint of its first president, the late Dr. Franklin Clark Fry, who was also its chief architect.

Its birth was marked by a dramatic ceremony in Detroit's Cobo Hall on June 28, 1962, when four quarters of a massive white candle, each with a separate wick, were lighted by acolytes and then moved together to form a single light, symbolizing union of the four merging bodies.

The four were the American Evangelical Lutheran Church (of Danish background), the Augustana Lutheran Church (of Swedish origin), the Finnish Evangelical Lutheran Church (with roots in Finland), and the United Lutheran Church in America (of German background, but with most of its members long assimilated into the mainstream of American life).

* * *

The United Lutheran Church contributed 25 million members, or more than three-fourths of the membership in the LCA. It was itself a product of a merger and was organized in 1918 through union of the General Synod of the Evangelical Lutheran Church in the U.S.A. (1820), the General Council of the Evangelical Lutheran Church in North America (1867), and the United Synod of the Evangelical Lutheran Church in the South (1886), successor to the General Synod of the Evangelical Lutheran Church in the Confederate States of America (1863).

The latter two bodies had separated from the General Synod in the 1860s over confessional issues, church polity, and the Civil War.

Efforts to reunite the three were spurred by the 400th anniversary of the Reformation, by joint efforts for a common liturgy and hymnal, by a translation of Luther's Small Catechism, and by cooperation on the foreign mission field.

One of the ULCA's constituent synods, the Ministerium of Pennsylvania, was the first synodical organization formed in America. It was organized in 1748 by Henry Melchior Muhlenberg, the patriarch of Lutheranism in America, and by other pastors sent from Halle, Germany, to minister to German colonists in North America.

As the colonists pushed west, north, and south, the Ministerium became the mother of other synods. One of them was the Central Pennsylvania Synod, known for its "low-church" character and for its ecumenical pioneering. It helped found the Pennsylvania Council of Churches in 1911.

The thrifty Pennsylvanians were responsible for an unusual development in ecumenism. More than 100 rural ULCA churches shared buildings with Reformed congregations and were known as union churches. Usually each pastor had two or more congregations, and if the congregations were small, they had union choirs, union Sunday schools, and other organizations in common. No union congregations were organized after 1900.

A vigorous home mission program resulted in the founding of more congregations and synods, but the ULCA remained a predominately eastern church with about 40% of its strength in Muhlenberg's state—Pennsylvania. Although English, German, and Dutch predominated, some 15 languages were used by ULCA congregations. Two ULCA synods were organized on the basis of language—Icelandic and Slovak.

When the ULCA was founded, disciplinary authority was left with the synods, as was authority to admit or remove pastors and ownership and control of seminaries, colleges, social service, and other institutions.

Some synods and seminaries reflected a more conservative theology than others, and there were differences in practice, including whether pastors could belong to secret orders, a highly controversial issue in some sections of Lutheranism.

One ULCA synod (Northwest) tried three of its pastors for heresy, with two found guilty and the third acquitted but advised to leave his congregation. Had they been in certain other ULCA synods, it is doubtful whether there would have been any trials.

Emphasis on social ministry was also characteristic of the ULCA, a tradition fostered by William A. Passavant, founder of hospitals and orphanages and a pioneer in introducing deaconess work in this country.

In a 1920 declaration the ULCA set forth fundamental principles on ecumenical relations, insisting that agreement in doctrine was needed for organic union but encouraging cooperation with other Christian groups if such cooperation did not compromise its testimony to what it held to be the truth.

The ULCA established a consultative relationship with the old Federal Council of Churches and became a full member of its successor, the National Council of Churches. ULCA representatives repeatedly insisted that ecumenical organizations be comprised only of official representatives named by the churches themselves—a principle later incorporated into the National and World Councils of Churches. It also insisted that ecumenical agencies be evangelical—comprised only of churches confessing Jesus Christ as Lord and Savior.

Franklin Clark Fry, who became president of the ULCA in 1944, succeeding Frederick H. Knubel (president from 1918 to 1944), helped organize both the NCC and WCC, serving as chairman of the Central and Executive Committees of the latter organization.

* * *

The Augustana Evangelical Lutheran Church, with some 500,000 members, was the second largest of the four bodies constituting the LCA. A colony of New Sweden was established in 1638 along the banks of the Delaware River. It was served by a succession of 35 clergymen, including the first regular Lutheran minister in America, Pastor Reorus Torkillus, who arrived with the first settlers.

Two centuries later, after the Revolution, when the Church of Sweden no longer provided clergymen, the congregations were absorbed into the Episcopal Church, the established communion of the English colonies.

Beginning about 1820 and continuing through the century, more than a million Swedes came to the United States, most of them settling in the central and upper Mississippi River Valley. Arriving with the immigrants in 1849 was Pastor Lars Paul Esbjorn, who established his headquarters in Andover, Ill., where he organized the First Swedish Lutheran Church in 1850. On a trip east that summer Pastor Esbjorn met the famed "Swedish Nightingale," Jennie Lind, who was so impressed with the needs he described that she gave $1500 to the cause.

Pastor Esbjorn established a number of preaching stations and organized several congregations. As immigrants continued to arrive, he appealed to Sweden for help. Several able pastors responded, and congregations were soon organized in Indiana, Illinois, Iowa, Minnesota, New York, and Pennsylvania.

Some Norwegian congregations of the Midwest joined forces to form the United Scandinavian Conference, which affiliated with the Synod of Northern Illinois of the General Synod. Because of theological differences within the synod, the Scandinavian Conference separated from the synod in 1860 and established an independent synod and seminary.

The Augustana Evangelical Lutheran Church was constituted in 1860 at the Norwegian Lutheran Church at Jefferson Prairie, Wis., by delegates from 36 Swedish and 13 Norwegian congregations. Augustana was the Latinized form of Augsburg, which refers to the confession of faith presented by Luther's colleagues at Augsburg, Germany. Augustana's first president was T. N. Hasselquist.

Augustana Seminary was started in Chicago as a continuation of a Scandinavian professorship that the United Scandinavian Conference began in 1858 at Springfield, Ill., and later moved to Paxton and Rock Island, Ill.

In 1870 the Norwegian element of the Augustana Synod asked to be released from further membership in order to carry on a more concentrated home mission program among the thousands of Norwegians thronging America. The request was granted cordially.

Also in 1870 Augustana voted to accept membership in the General Council and to cooperate with other Lutheran bodies in evangelism. Until 1905 it supported the General Council's foreign mission program in India and Puerto Rico.

An Augustana pastor, Eric Norelius, founded the first Swedish Lutheran orphanage at Vasa, Minn., in 1865. In 1884 the first hospital was started under Augustana auspices in Chicago.

During the terms of its last three presidents, P. O. Bersell, Oscar Benson, and Malvin Lundeen, Augustana strove for Lutheran union on the largest possible scale and became a pioneer member of ecumenical and inter-Lutheran organizations.

* * *

The Finnish Evangelical Lutheran Church, also known as the Suomi Synod, contributed some 30,000 members to the LCA.

It was founded in 1890 in Calumet, Mich., by nine congregations served by pastors who had migrated from Finland, and was patterned after the state church of the homeland. It opened its door to all who accepted the Lutheran confessions of faith, although the Finnish language was used almost exclusively in the early years.

Dr. J.K. Nikander, father of the synod, was the guiding light through the early years. Working with people scattered through Michigan, hampered by snow and poor roads, and bitterly opposed by Communist agitators, the early clergy of the Suomi Synod found life difficult and results meager.

Some dissatisfied members founded their own church organization, the Finnish National Lutheran Church, which later affiliated with the Lutheran Church–Missouri Synod.

In 1896 Suomi College and Theological Seminary opened its doors in Hancock, Mich.

For many years the ULCA supported the Suomi Synod's home mission work, and in Canada Finnish congregations joined the ULCA's Canada Synod.

The Suomi Synod's last two presidents were John Wargelin and his son, Raymond W.

*   *   *

The American Evangelical Lutheran Church, smallest of the LCA merging bodies with some 20,000 members, was known as the Danish Evangelical Lutheran Church in America until it changed its name in 1954.

The "happy Danes," as they were called, had their beginning as a church body in 1871 when four pastors met in Neenah, Wis., and organized the Church Missionary Society, the forerunner of the AELC. Two of the pastors had come from Denmark after Claus Laurits Clausen, founder of the Norwegian congregation that was the germ of what became the ELC, had called for help in church work among Danish immigrants in America.

More pastors came from Denmark, more congregations were organized in the Midwest, and the future of the new group looked promising. But the group split in 1894 in controversy over several questions, including whether the Bible is or contains the Word of God.

The minority—pietists close to Denmark's Inner Mission movement—organized what they called the North Church and merged with another Danish group two years later to form what later became the United Evangelical Lutheran Church (now a part of the ALC).

The majority, often called "Grundtvigians" after the famous leader in Denmark, remained in what was later called the AELC. They established their headquarters in Des Moines, Iowa, where they opened Grand View College and Seminary in 1896.

Closely related to the AELC congregations were folk schools giving short courses mostly for farm men and women and also serving as Americanization schools for the constant stream of immigrants.

The AELC long supported the Santal Mission in India with funds and personnel.

Dr. Alfred Jensen served as AELC president from 1936 to 1960.

* * *

The merger creating the LCA has taken well, in the judgment of observers.

When Fry died in 1968, he was succeeded by Dr. Robert J. Marshall, a former seminary professor who was president of the LCA's Illinois Synod. His calm, reserved leadership style was a marked change from Fry's flamboyance.

Under the leadership of Fry and Marshall, the LCA succeeded in breaking out of Lutheran pietism into greater social involvement without losing its churchly character.

A document called the Manifesto, encouraging congregation self-study, led LCA members to increased consciousness about urban ministry. In the past decade, the ACT (Act in Crisis Today) appeal has raised funds for creative new approaches in crisis centers. New congregations have been started among black and Hispanic people, and there are clusters of LCA inner-city congregations.

In May 1969 the LCA headquarters in New York City was one of the first denominational offices visited by the black militant James Forman in behalf of the Black Economic Development Conference. He taped to the door of the LCA office building the BEDC manifesto, which demanded $500 million from America's churches as "reparations" to black people.

President Marshall listened to Forman's statement and promised to study the demand for $50 million from the LCA, but made no comment.

At its 1968 convention, the LCA became the first major Protestant body to uphold selective conscientious objection to a particular war.

Over the years, LCA conventions also have approved social statements dealing with religious liberty; social welfare; capital punishment; poverty; the war in Vietnam; sex, marriage, and the family; world community; the correctional system; and the crisis in ecology.

The LCA has not been satisfied to stick to its inherited patterns and ways of doing things.

For example, it was the first Lutheran body to drop the idea of separate youth and men's organizations on the national level. Behind the move was a desire to incorporate youth and men into the total life of LCA congregations.

And at its 1970 convention in Minneapolis, the LCA became the first Lutheran body in North America to authorize the ordination of women to its ministry.

The first woman ordained by the LCA (and by any

17

North American Lutheran body) was the Rev. Elizabeth A. Platz, 30, a lay Lutheran chaplain at the University of Maryland. By April 1978 the LCA had ordained 58 women, 40 of whom were serving as parish pastors. LCA seminaries also had a large proportion of woman students.

The consciousness-raising efforts of an LCA committee on women in church and society and an LCA women's caucus produced tangible results. At the 1976 convention, 20 women were elected to the LCA executive council, management committees, and boards. Many revisions were made in official publications and documents, deleting "sexist" language.

The growing participation of LCA women in their congregations and synods can be seen in the growing proportion of women delegates to LCA conventions. For example, 43% of lay delegates elected to the 1978 LCA convention in Chicago were women. In addition, 4 of the 344 clergy delegates were women.

One effect of the decision to ordain women has been to decrease the number of women who have gone into the diaconate. Another has been to give the LCA almost as many ministers as it needs.

Like other Protestant denominations, the LCA spent many years working out a restructuring of its organization. The LCA restructuring, done at the prompting of President Marshall, produced a managerial style that filtered down to the synods and other parts of the church.

Not everyone regards the restructuring as an unqualified success. Said one observer: "It (the restructuring) made the Division for Parish Services and the Division for Mission in North America into conglomerates, with the result that some people feel certain functions of the church are being neglected or placed down at a third level of administration."

For much of the past decade, LCA benevolences have not kept pace with inflation. The result has been cutbacks in the number of mission congregations begun and mission personnel sent overseas, and reduction of national staff and numerous programs. An intensified Christian giving program in the late 1970s appeared to be helping the church reverse this trend.

A Strength for Mission Appeal, with a minimum goal of $25 million and a maximum goal of $40 million, was conducted by the LCA in 1978. By midyear a total of $34.4 million had been given or committed, and there were good prospects the maximum goal might eventually be attained.

Bulk of the money raised in the appeal was to be used for mission development in North America and world mission. A total of $1 million was allocated to fund an intensified program for Christian giving to enable the LCA to achieve a minimum budget level of $50 million annually in benevolent giving by 1980. Another $1 million was to be used for mission on the congregational level.

Over the years the LCA has conducted a number of other appeals, including the Love Compels Action and World Hunger Appeals, which raised millions for overseas relief and domestic concerns.

The LCA was one of some 50 U.S. and Canadian denominations participating in Key '73, the year of evangelism in 1973. At the invitation of the American Lutheran Church, it also participated in Evangelical Outreach, a cooperative evangelism emphasis begun in 1977.

The LCA also was a partner in the inter-Lutheran commission that produced the *Lutheran Book of Worship*.

19

It also joined the ALC in drafting a joint statement on communion practices.

Increasingly, the LCA has moved toward closer cooperation and even consolidation in its programs of theological and college education. The LCA's Northwestern Seminary was relocated from Minneapolis to the campus of the ALC's Luther Seminary in St. Paul, and since 1976 the two seminaries have been operating with "maximal functional" unity, sharing a president, a dean of academic affairs, a dean of students, and a business manager. The two seminaries in 1978 had 831 students, making St. Paul the largest center of Lutheran theological education in North America.

In another development, two Ohio institutions—the LCA's Hamma School of Theology at Springfield and the ALC's Seminary in Columbus—were consolidated under the name of Trinity Lutheran Seminary and began joint operation on the Columbus campus in late 1978.

Earlier, the LCA's seminary in Saskatoon, Canada, was merged with the former ALC seminary there.

The LCA, early in its history, merged five seminaries of its four constituent bodies into the new Lutheran School of Theology on a new campus near the University of Chicago. The seminaries were Augustana, Maywood, Suomi, Grand View, and Central.

Efforts to consolidate the LCA's Gettysburg and Philadelphia seminaries in Pennsylvania have not succeeded, but the two have become related through the LCA Council for Lutheran Theological Education in the Northeast. Another proposal for their future is to be made by 1986.

The LCA also supports a seminary in Berkeley, Calif., with which the ALC cooperates, and another in Waterloo, Canada.

Through its synods, the LCA is associated with 22 colleges. Of these, 18 are LCA, one is jointly operated with the ALC, two are ALC, and two are of the Evangelical Lutheran Church of Canada.

Three of the LCA colleges—Augustana, Gettysburg, and Muhlenberg—have chapters in Phi Beta Kappa honor society. Gettysburg, founded in 1832, is the oldest Lutheran college in the United States. Waterloo University in Canada, which was the largest LCA school, became a government-supported provincial school in the early 1970s and is no longer related to the LCA.

The LCA, through "seed money" grants, has provided overseas projects at many of the colleges. Several of the colleges operate special programs to aid minority group youths.

The LCA, through its Division for Mission in North America, has had many unusual ministries. For example, Dr. John G. Gensel serves as a missionary to the "jazz community of New York City." In Cleveland, Ohio, a storefront church ministers to street people.

On the overseas scene, the LCA has gone through a fundamental shift in mission strategy. The church was once related to its overseas "mission fields" in a parent-child relationship. The overseas churches (in Latin America, Africa, India, Japan, Taiwan, Indonesia, Malaysia, and Hong Kong) are now becoming self-supporting and the LCA relates to them as partner rather than as parent. The change accommodates the growing nationalism overseas and the increase of indigenous leadership. Good missionaries always work themselves out of a job by training others to take their place.

A new parish education curriculum developed by the LCA in the 1960s was "an aggiornamento" (a bringing up to date) for the denomination, according to President Marshall.

The Lutheran, LCA organ, long has enjoyed the highest paid circulation of any denominational publication, with subscriptions approaching the 600,000 mark. It is widely regarded as one of the best church publications in the country. The LCA's Fortress Press, which publishes about 50 books a year, also is highly regarded.

The LCA has been open to other Christian denominations to a degree that no other Lutheran group in America has. At the same time, it has sought the closest possible relations with other Lutheran bodies.

However, in 1978 it rejected a proposal from the Lutheran Church–Missouri Synod that the two bodies hold "bilateral discussions" on doctrinal issues. The LCA said it preferred the multilateral discussions conducted for several years under auspices of the Lutheran Council in the U.S.A. as a way of achieving theological consensus with the LCMS.

The LCMS had suggested that it might establish altar and pulpit fellowship with the LCA if doctrinal agreement could be reached. However, LCA President Marshall pointed out that "for the LCA no further discussion or agreement is required, since the LCMS subscribes to the Unaltered Augsburg Confession and Luther's Small Catechism, which are the basis on which the LCA recognizes other churches to be in faith with it."

According to its constitution, the LCA anchors its oneness in the confession of "Jesus Christ as the Lord of the Church," acknowledges the Holy Scriptures as "the norm for the faith and life of the Church," and believes the Scriptures are the "divinely inspired record of God's redemptive act in Christ."

President Marshall, who became head of the LCA in

1968 on Fry's death and who was re-elected in 1970 and 1974 by big majorities, stunned the LCA constituency when he announced in March 1978 that he would not be a candidate for re-election at the 1978 convention.

Marshall, then 59, announced he would become director of the Office of Mission, Service and Development of Lutheran World Ministries, a cooperative organization for the LCA, the American Lutheran Church, and the Association of Evangelical Lutheran Churches.

"I decided that an opportune time had arrived for a transition," he said in a letter to the denominational officers. "It is a time of opportunity when the church can benefit from the fresh energies of new leadership."

There was an outpouring of praise for Marshall as strong leader of the LCA and also key contributor to the Lutheran World Federation, the World Council of Churches, and the National Council of Churches over the past decade.

"The uniqueness of his contribution," said Dr. Paul A. Wee, general secretary of Lutheran World Ministries, "lies in his ability to combine professional managerial skills with the prophetic thrust of the gospel message and the shepherding concern of a parish pastor. Those who have worked closely with him are aware of the significant role he has played in establishing basic policy directions for the world family of Christian churches."

The LCA, at its 1978 convention in Chicago, elected Dr. James R. Crumley Jr. as president to succeed Marshall. Crumley, who had been LCA secretary for four years, was named on the sixth ballot, receiving 337 votes—one more than necessary.

The runner-up was Dr. William H. Lazareth, director of the LCA's Department of Church and Society, who led Crumley in total votes on each of the first five ballots.

Ironically, Crumley also came from behind to win the church secretary post on a fourth ballot at the LCA convention in Baltimore in 1974. In that contest also, Lazareth was his closest competitor.

On the first ballot for president at the 1978 convention, 70 candidates received votes. Dr. H. George Anderson, president of Lutheran Theological Southern Seminary at Columbia, S.C., outdistanced all competitors with 244 votes, but pulled himself out of the contest before the second ballot.

Crumley, who "grew up in a small rural congregation in the hills of Tennessee," came to the LCA secretaryship from a pastorate in Savannah, Ga. During an earlier pastorate in Oak Ridge, Tenn., he had in his congregation many scientists from the Oak Ridge National Laboratory. "I saw that the problems of Ph.D.s were the same as the problems of the people back in the hills," he said following his election.

Elected to succeed Crumley as LCA secretary was Dr. Reuben T. Swanson, president of the LCA's Nebraska Synod.

The Lutheran Church-Missouri Synod

CONCERN for "pure doctrine" has dominated much of the history of the Lutheran Church–Missouri Synod, the nation's second largest Lutheran body.

Often this concern has led to sharp controversy, such as occurred in the late 1970s when a split developed over Bible interpretation and teaching at the synod's major seminary, eventually prompting some synod "moderates" to leave and form a new seminary and denomination.

The outcome was hailed as a triumph for Lutheran orthodoxy, marking the first time, it was claimed, that the trend to liberalism in a major Protestant denomination had been reversed.

This interpretation may be an oversimplification, because the controversy in the 1970s, like that of others earlier in the synod's history, was not only theological, but also involved clashing personalities and power struggles.

Nevertheless, strict allegiance to conservative and confessional Lutheranism has been a hallmark of the Missouri Synod since its organization in Chicago in 1847 as "Die

Deutsche Evangelisch-Lutherische Synode von Missouri, Ohio und anderen Staaten."

The founders of the Lutheran Church–Missouri Synod (the name adopted in 1947) were Saxons from Germany who were looking for a place where they could "enjoy, without interference, the complete and unadulterated means of grace ordained by God for all men unto salvation" and could "preserve in their integrity and purity for themselves and their children."

Led by Pastor Martin Stephan of Dresden, some 700 of them sailed for the United States in late 1838 (one ship was lost at sea) and came up the Mississippi River to Missouri.

Later groups, in sympathy with the first, also came to Missouri. Pastor Stephan was found to be too autocratic for the new settlers, who deposed him and expelled him from the settlement.

The mantle of leadership then fell upon Pastor C.F.W. Walther, who was elected first president when the synod was organized in 1847 by 12 congregations and 22 ministers at First St. Paul's Church, Chicago.

The German name chosen reflected the synod's German constituency. The synod's official language was German.

The early leaders sent missionaries to all parts of North America and established schools to train pastors and teachers. A log cabin college-seminary erected in Perry County, Missouri, in 1839, was the forerunner of all LCMS educational institutions. It was moved to St. Louis in 1849 when its first president, Pastor Walther, began his long career at Concordia Seminary. The chief architect of the LCMS theological position was Franz Pieper, a long-time professor at the St. Louis seminary. Closely allied with this school was another Concordia Seminary, located first in Fort Wayne,

Ind., then in Springfield, Ill., and more recently back in Fort Wayne.

The LCMS today also operates 14 colleges in the United States (most of them named "Concordia") that prepare students for teaching careers or give them pre-seminary training. Graduates of the synod's teachers' colleges staff the 1200 Christian day schools operated by LCMS congregations, which constitute the largest parochial school system of any American Protestant denomination. The synod-sponsored kindergarten-through-seminary educational system has fostered a cohesiveness and esprit de corps in the denomination.

Valparaiso University in Valparaiso, Ind., is affiliated with the LCMS, but not owned directly by it. Some synod congregations contribute to the support of the university, which, with nearly 5000 students, is the nation's largest Lutheran educational institution.

Besides education, the LCMS has long been known for its social ministry. It began in 1868 at DePeres, Mo., with an orphanage to serve children brought back by returning Civil War veterans. Today the synod has a host of institutional chaplaincies and health and welfare agencies. Beginning in the 1960s and 1970s, LCMS districts joined with jurisdictions of other Lutheran bodies in operating Lutheran social service agencies. At its 1967 convention, the synod launched an ambitious program for open housing, setting up a system of loans and grants to be used in helping minorities find places to live.

The LCMS has made a strong effort to work in the South and in the inner city and has the largest number of black clergymen and members of any U.S. Lutheran body. LCMS congregations in 1978 observed the synod's centennial thankoffering to be used in aiding black students preparing for pastoral ministry. The 1977 synod convention adopted the goal of recruiting and educating 150 black pastors in the following 10 years.

An unofficial organization, the Lutheran Human Relations Association, begun by LCMS members, has long prodded the synod membership to concern itself with problems of racial minorities. Several years ago, the association opened its membership to all Lutherans.

Medical missions, missions to the deaf, and mass-media ministries are other areas in which the LCMS has pioneered. The Lutheran Hour, which had its first network broadcast in 1930, is aired over more than 1000 U.S. radio stations, and in other formats abroad, using indigenous personnel. The Lutheran Laymen's League, sponsors, estimates the weekly listening audience of all its programs, which are broadcast in 46 languages, at 40 million. The Lutheran Hour program, which seeks to "bring Christ to the nations," long featured the late Walter A. Maier as its preacher. In recent years, the preacher has been Oswald C.J. Hoffmann, former LCMS public relations director, whose work on behalf of the American Bible Society led to his election as president of the worldwide United Bible Societies.

Through the Lutheran Laymen's League, the LCMS also sponsors a half-hour television drama series in full color, called "This Is the Life," started in 1952. In 1978, it was being carried by about 160 U.S. television stations and by others in some 40 countries abroad.

Another project of the Laymen's League has been to sponsor "Preaching Through the Press," display advertisements in major Sunday newspaper supplements and other publications.

The American Lutheran Publicity Bureau was founded

by LCMS clergymen to help Lutheran congregations with their public relations. The LCMS itself long has had a highly organized public relations network extending into its districts. Concordia Publishing House, St. Louis, the synod's publishing arm, is one of the nation's leading church-owned publishing houses. The synod's main publications are "The Reporter," a weekly newsletter for church leaders, and *The Lutheran Witness,* a magazine.

An aggressive mission policy, coupled with the conviction that "we've got the truth," made the LCMS for many years the fastest-growing of the major Lutheran bodies. But in the 1970s growth slowed somewhat, partly because of the falling birth rate and partly because of the doctrinal split. The LCMS world mission fields include the Caribbean, Africa, Sri Lanka (Ceylon), Hong Kong, India, Japan, Korea, the Middle East, New Guinea, the Philippines, and Taiwan.

Over the years, relations with other Lutheran bodies often have provided stormy episodes in the life of the LCMS.

It was Walther's hope that there could be "one united Evangelical Lutheran Church of North America." This didn't materialize, but the Evangelical Lutheran Synodical Conference of North America was founded in 1872 by several of the confessionally-minded synods, including Missouri.

Two of the synods withdrew in the 1880s in a controversy over the doctrines of election and conversion. There was more controversy in the middle of this century as the LCMS sought to establish fellowship with German synods that later formed the old American Lutheran Church.

At convention after convention Missouri Synod delegates debated Romans 16:17 ("Now I beseech you, brethren, mark them which cause divisions and offences contrary to the doctrine which ye have learned: and avoid them") in relation to the proposed "common confession" being negotiated with the old ALC.

The controversies and attacks on other Lutheran groups became so bitter that in 1945 a committee of 44 pastors and professors of the synod issued a statement deploring the "loveless" and legalistic attitude of the synod and the barriers people constructed hindering the free course of the gospel in the world.

Partly as a result of their plea, the synod began to permit joint prayer with Lutherans with whom it was not in fellowship. Other principles advocated by the 44 also were later adopted or tolerated.

Eventually the Wisconsin and Evangelical Lutheran Synods protested the Missouri Synod's growing relations with bodies not in the synodical Conference, and they suspended fellowship with the Missouri Synod and withdrew from the conference.

After the present ALC was formed in 1960, the Missouri Synod resumed fellowship discussions with the enlarged body, and its 1967 convention in New York adopted a resolution declaring that the scriptural and confessional basis for fellowship with the ALC "exists." The synod's president was asked to "make the appropriate recommendations" to the 1969 convention.

In the 1967-69 biennium more discussions were carried on with the ALC—from the top level of officials to the grassroots. Critics of the fellowship proposal aimed their fire at the ALC's allegedly liberal view of Scripture, the ALC's ecumenical relations, and its attitude toward lodgery.

At the synod's 1969 convention in Denver, President Harms, in conjunction with the synod's Council of Presidents, submitted a resolution declaring meetings of congregations, pastors, and officials "generally confirmed the conclusion that the scriptural and confessional basis for church fellowship exists."

The resolution, which called upon the Synod formally to declare itself to be in altar and pulpit fellowship with the ALC, infuriated synod conservatives and rightists.

In advance of the convention *The Christian News,* a right-wing weekly that had carried on a long campaign against progressives in the synod, called for defeat of President Harms and threw its support to Dr. Jacob (Jack) A.O. Preus, president of Concordia Seminary, Springfield, Ill.

Several elements in the synod joined together to support Preus and came to Denver with a full slate of candidates, including nominees for synod boards and conventions. For means of mutual identification, they wore lapel pins in the form of a fish hook, long a symbol of an evangelist or a personal worker for Christ.

On the first day of the convention, Dr. Walter F. Wolbrecht, the synod's executive director, angrily attacked the campaign for Preus.

"Never before in the annals of the Missouri Synod has there been an open, avowed, and public candidacy for the top office of the church body weeks in advance of an electing convention," Wolbrecht said. He cited a paid advertisement in behalf of Preus that appeared in a Denver newspaper on the eve of the convention.

Preus, given the convention floor to respond, said that nobody runs for the presidency of the synod, that he was no more a candidate than any other of its pastors. He said the newspaper advertisement and the articles in *The Christian News* promoting his candidacy were without his prior knowledge or consent.

Preus, 49, unseated Harms, 67, in the second ballot after the nominating ballot. Preus became the first person of non-German background to be elected to the synod presidency in its 122-year history. His background is almost 100% Norwegian, although he pointed out at a post-election press conference that "Preus means Prussian."

After Preus's election many observers expected that the convention would defeat the resolution to declare fellowship with the ALC. Preus, a graduate of an ALC college and an ALC seminary, who was ordained in a predecessor body of the ALC, and who has four uncles and four cousins who are ALC pastors, told the convention he favored "a delay in declaring fellowship at this time," but promised to abide by the convention's decision and "to procure consensus and fellowship with all Lutherans in America with all vigor and sincerity."

An all-day preconvention hearing and parts of three plenary sessions were devoted to the fellowship question. On the evening of July 16, delegates took a secret ballot vote on the recommendation resolving that "with joy and praise the synod herewith declare itself to be in altar and pulpit fellowship with the American Lutheran Church."

When the result—a 522 to 438 vote for fellowship—was announced the next morning, spontaneous applause broke out mingled with cheers. Then the delegates and visitors sang "O God, our help in ages past."

The outcome was a vindication of Harms's stand on fellowship, but some conservatives refused to accept it and made plans for a national meeting to work to rescind the action in 1971.

Fellowship, when formally declared in effect, was intended to make possible an exchange of pulpits and intercommunion for members of the two bodies, and to facilitate transfer of members between bodies, but not all LCMS congregations practiced it.

In a corollary action the Denver convention approved fellowship with the Evangelical Lutheran Church of Canada, a former district of the ALC.

In view of the fellowship vote, many delegates were hopeful that the synod would decide to join the Lutheran World Federation at its Denver convention. However, Preus urged the convention to delay seeking LWF membership, and in a minority report he and two other signers listed objections to the LWF. They contended that the LWF permits "conflicting views regarding authority, inspiration and inerrancy of the Scriptures in the various member churches"; that it is "intimately associated with the World Council of Churches"; that it has "churchly features and functions"; that its intercommunion practices are "not soundly Lutheran," and that cost of membership could be "very great."

Delegates voted 272 to 620 against a recommendation that it apply for LWF membership. It was the second time that the Missouri Synod had turned down LWF membership. The first time was in 1956. The Synod is the largest Lutheran body not in the federation, which embraces 52 million of the world's estimated 75 million Lutherans.

The Denver convention did vote to keep the synod in the Lutheran Council in the U.S.A., which it helped organize, but rejected an "open end" appeal for relief and inner city mission needs to be conducted under the council's auspices.

Delegates voted for continued discussions with the Lutheran Church in America (LCA) and with the LCA's Canadian districts, with a view toward establishing fellowship with those bodies.

Merger of the 20,500-member Synod of Evangelical Lutheran Churches (SELC) into the LCMS was approved by the Denver convention. Under the agreement, later approved by SELC at its convention, the SELC was to become a district of the LCMS for seven years, after which it was to be dissolved and the congregations, pastors, and teachers of the district assigned to geographical districts of the LCMS.

In another significant decision the 1969 convention—which was all-male, like all earlier synod conventions—agreed that "Scripture does not prohibit women from exercising the franchise in congregational or synodical assemblies." The action opened the way for women to serve on local and synodical boards, commissions, and committees, and as delegates to synod conventions. However, it specifically barred women from holding pastoral office.

Blacks and youth made a strong impact on the Denver convention. Some 30 blacks, mostly young people, marched into the convention hall during one session and made a moving presentation of their hopes and desires for their church. Spokesmen presented six demands and paid tribute to pioneer black clergy in the synod. About 500 delegates and visitors later followed the blacks outside for a brief rally. In response to one of the demands, the convention voted to grant a sum of up to $1 million for capital needs for the synod's academy and college in Selma, Ala., a predominately black institution.

The synod affirmed the "legitimacy" of black power, authorized youth to become nonvoting representatives at future conventions, reaffirmed the acceptability of federal funds for children attending nonpublic schools, and called for recognition of conscientious objectors to specific wars.

Besides the synod presidency, another key synod office was filled in 1969—the presidency of Concordia Seminary, St. Louis, where Dr. A.O. Fuerbringer retired. Named to succeed him was Dr. John H. Tietjen, former director of public relations for the Lutheran Council in the U.S.A., who was expected to exercise strong leadership in the direction of great ecumenical involvement for the LCMS, including LWF membership.

But Tietjen had been president of Concordia Seminary only a few months when Preus announced establishment of a "fact-finding" committee to investigate the teaching at the seminary, in particular the use of the historical-critical method of Bible interpretation.

The faculty protested the investigation, which led the American Association of Theological Schools in 1972 to place the seminary on probation for two years.

Later in 1972, Preus issued a 160-page report to the synod, detailing the findings of the investigating committee and declaring that the LCMS was at a doctrinal crossroads.

Tietjen followed with a 35-page report, calling the Preus report "unfair, untrue, sub-biblical and unLutheran."

The faculty rejected the Preus report and the seminary board of control commended the faculty.

Preus took the controversy to the 1973 LCMS convention in New Orleans. By a 58% majority, the delegates declared, in effect, that Tietjen and 45 of his 50 faculty members were guilty of teaching "false doctrine which cannot be tolerated in the church of God, much less excused or defended."

Tietjen and his professors were condemned for accepting a widely used scholarly framework allowing many Bible stories to be interpreted symbolically—Adam and Eve, Jonah and the big fish, the Israelites crossing the Red Sea, and some New Testament accounts.

The New Orleans convention also adopted as a synodical doctrinal position a document composed by Preus a year earlier, "A Statement of Scriptural and Confessional Principles."

The convention referred charges against Tietjen to the seminary board of control, which had come under control of conservatives and which early in 1974 suspended him. The seminary students declared a moratorium on classes to protest the suspension, and the faculty majority and staff served notice they would not return until their teaching was recognized as in accord with LCMS doctrinal standards.

On February 19, most of the seminary students decided not to return to classes and they left the campus to form Seminex (Concordia Seminary in Exile). Classes began the next day in facilities of the Divinity School of St. Louis University (Roman Catholic) and Eden Seminary (United Church of Christ).

Whether Seminex graduates could be placed in LCMS congregations occupied the synod's attention for many months. Preus urged all district presidents not to ordain or install Seminex graduates until they could be examined and approved by his representatives.

In late 1974 the Concordia Board of Control formally terminated Tietjen as Concordia president, finding him guilty of 10 charges of false doctrine and malfeasance.

Meanwhile, the synod's controversy reached its missions operations, with several staff officials resigning to protest "oppressive politics" of the LCMS Board for Missions. The Hong Kong mission, for example, was split.

Several meetings were held, looking toward reconciliation between synod officials and "moderates" who in 1973 organized Evangelical Lutherans in Mission (ELIM).

The 1975 LCMS convention in Anaheim, Calif., asked those taking active role in the "schismatic functions" of ELIM either to cease leadership, disassociate themselves from ELIM as long as it continues such functions, or, in conscience, terminate membership in the LCMS.

The convention asked professors, students, and supporters of Seminex to close the institution and said district presidents who had ordained or placed unauthorized Seminex graduates should seek to have them authorized or resign their offices.

In April 1976 Preus removed four district presidents from office for continuing to ordain Seminex graduates. He named acting presidents to fill the vacancies.

In December 1976 LCMS "moderates" officially constituted the Association of Evangelical Lutheran Churches (AELC), joining together five new regional synods they had organized earlier.

Many congregations and pastors joined the AELC but continued to keep their membership also in the LCMS. The 1977 synod convention in Dallas decided that congregations must terminate their membership in the AELC no later than 30 days before the conventions of their districts in 1978 or forfeit their LCMS membership.

The Dallas convention elected Preus to his third term as president.

The LCMS in Dallas made three decisions affecting other Lutheran bodies.

It voted to declare a "state of fellowship in protest" with the American Lutheran Church, citing differences with the ALC over whether women should be ordained, on interpreting the Bible, and on association with non-Lutheran groups.

In another decision, the LCMS voted to stay in the Lutheran Council in the U.S.A.

And in the third action, the synod refused to approve plans to publish the *Lutheran Book of Worship,* calling instead for a "blue-ribbon committee" to examine the contents of the book "in light of many theological questions." (The LCMS had been responsible for forming the inter-Lutheran commission that prepared the joint hymnal-service book.)

In a postconvention development, Tietjen, who had become president of Christ Seminary–Seminex, as the breakaway seminary became known, was removed from the synod's clergy roster after he was found guilty by a synod official of "holding and defending, allowing and fostering false doctrines."

With the synod's first major schism behind him, Preus told the 1977 convention that the LCMS was about to enter a peaceful era after several years of turmoil.

The split, Preus said in 1978, was "sad and unfortunate, certainly—but minimal compared to the dire predictions of the size of the split from the synod made a few years back."

The final report of LCMS statistics for 1977 showed baptized membership for the year had declined by 86,616 to 2.7 million, and the number of congregations had declined 111 to 6051.

Preus noted, however, that LCMS contributions reached an all-time high of $366.6 million in 1977, with per communicant giving—the highest of the major Lutheran bodies —increasing to $178.66.

Suggestions that the LCMS might retreat into its former

isolation have been rejected by Preus, who noted that the LCMS has invited all Lutheran bodies to have bilateral doctrinal discussions. There seemed the possibility that the LCMS, under Preus' leadership, might seek to renew fellowship with such former allies as the Wisconsin Evangelical Lutheran Synod and the Evangelical Lutheran Synod. A break in fellowship with the ALC would facilitate the renewal of ties with the LCMS' former partners in the now extinct Evangelical Lutheran Synodical Conference of North America.

Preus is the eighth president of the LCMS. His predecessors were C.F.W. Walther (1847-50 and 1864-78); F.C.D. Wyneken (1850-64); H.C. Schwan (1878-99); F.A.O. Pieper (1899-1911); F.B. Pfotenhauer (1911-35); J.W. Behnken (1935-62), and O.R. Harms (1962-69).

The American Lutheran Church

THE American Lutheran Church is often viewed as the "middle of the road" church in U.S. Lutheranism. It is a moderate church not given to extremes.

The ALC has a homogenous membership—mostly descendants of poor European immigrant stock who have lived out the American dream and made it on their own as self-achievers.

It is strongly Midwestern in orientation, with more than half of its 2.4 million members in five states: Minnesota, Iowa, Wisconsin, and the two Dakotas. Another 30% are in Ohio, Illinois, Michigan, California, Texas, and Washington.

The American Lutheran Church is a union of some 4800 congregations located in 47 states. (There are none in Connecticut, Rhode Island, and South Carolina.) The denomination began functioning in 1961, following the 1960 merger of the American Lutheran Church (German background), the Evangelical Lutheran Church (Norwegian background), and the United Evangelical Lutheran

Church (Danish background). The Lutheran Free Church (also of Norwegian background) came into the ALC in 1963 after the first two of three congregational referendums it conducted on joining the union failed. (About 40 LFC congregations decided not to enter the merged church and organized as an Association of Free Lutheran Congregations.)

Dr. Fredrik A. Schiotz, who headed the old ELC, was elected first president of the ALC, serving until 1971, the limit permitted under the constitution. Under his leadership, the merger congealed rapidly with the four ethnic churches becoming one strong body. From his own background of service with the younger churches in the Third World, Schiotz helped raise the international consciousness of the denomination. Recognition of his role as an international Lutheran leader came with his election as president of the Lutheran World Federation, a position he held from 1963 to 1970.

Schiotz also worked hard to bring about greater Lutheran unity in the United States and played an influential role in the creation of the Lutheran Council in the U.S.A. in 1966 with all three major Lutheran bodies participating, and in the 1969 decision of the Lutheran Church–Missouri Synod to accept altar and pulpit fellowship with the ALC. (The ALC and the Lutheran Church in America were already in fellowship.)

In 1970 Dr. Kent S. Knutson, one of the ALC's leading theologians (he had been a professor at Luther Seminary and president of Wartburg Seminary), was elected Schiotz' successor. His election climaxed several months of open campaigning that was unprecedented in U.S. Lutheranism. He was the youngest of 10 candidates nominated by the 18 ALC districts.

Knutson has been credited with strongly articulating the ALC's theological basis and helping to change its theological stance from defensive to positive.

He also led the ALC in restructuring itself, a plan intended to decentralize authority, which led to combining several ALC units.

But Knutson did not live to see his restructured plan completed. He died in 1973, at the age of 48, of Jakob-Creutzfeldt disease, a rare, fatal disorder of the central nervous system, which made it impossible for him to speak and communicate and which he was believed to have contracted in New Guinea.

Dr. David W. Preus, a Minneapolis pastor who was ALC vice-president and acting president, automatically succeeded Knutson on his death and set about to complete the restructuring of the ALC national offices. In 1974 Preus was elected to his first full term as ALC president.

The Preus' administration has been characterized by:

• Strong affirmation of congregations as centers for mission.

• Emphasis on living with theological diversity within the church's unity.

• An effort to stand with both feet in the world, combining an evangelical thrust with a stance for justice.

• A growing concern for justice on the international level, particularly in relation to southern Africa.

• A stance of greater cooperation, but not union at this time, in inter-Lutheran relationships.

Although Preus is a cousin of LCMS President J.A.O. Preus, relationships between the two bodies have deteriorated, partly because of LCMS insistence on theological uniformity with those with which it is in fellowship. The

LCMS voted at its 1977 convention to declare a state of "fellowship in protest" with the ALC.

Meanwhile, closer ties have developed between the ALC and the LCA. Especially significant has been the moving together of seminaries of the two church bodies in Minnesota and Ohio, and ALC support of an LCA seminary in California. The two bodies also have been cooperating in colleges, parish education, and the Evangelical Outreach program.

ALC and LCA representatives have been meeting together to study what could be done about differences in polity (church organization) and in developing compatible jurisdictional units with similar powers and functions.

With the LCMS and the Evangelical Lutheran Church of Canada, the ALC and the LCA cooperated in developing the *Lutheran Book of Worship,* published in 1978.

Growing involvement in social issues has characterized the ALC in recent years. In 1968 more than 90% of ALC congregations participated in Project Summer Hope, a four-month project to sensitize ALC members in the urban-racial crisis.

An episode that stirred considerable ALC reaction was the involvement of Dr. Paul Boe, then director of the ALC's Social Service Division, with the American Indian Movement during its occupation of Wounded Knee, S.D., in 1973. Boe was subpoenaed to testify before a federal grand jury in Sioux Falls, S.D., about what he had seen and heard in Wounded Knee. He refused. He believed the relationship of trust he had with the Indians would be betrayed if he testified.

Boe was ultimately sentenced to prison, but after national leaders and some of the nation's major religious bodies joined in a friend-of-the-court appeal, a circuit court of appeals overturned the sentence on a technicality and the issue of clergy confidentiality was not faced. When Boe's position in the ALC was phased out in restructuring, he began a new ministry, seeking to create better understanding of problems of the Indians.

ALC grants also helped start and maintain the controversial Program in Human Sexuality at the University of Minnesota Medical School to train persons in the helping professions. The program became controversial because of its use of sexually explicit films and the participation of homosexuals as lecturers. In 1977, after six years of experimentation, the ALC decided to conclude its participation in the "action research" phase of the program, but to continue on a committee that has aided the program by conducting a dialog between medicine and religion.

At its 1976 convention in Washington, the ALC approved a "Manifesto for Our Nation's Third Century" intended to be "a commentary on the 'American Dream' in light of the Gospel" and a spur to continued participation of the church in public affairs.

World hunger has been for many years a concern of ALC members, most of whom live in states that raise 25% of the world's food. A special ALC office directed attention to the problem. On Thanksgiving, 1976, for example, many congregations encouraged their members to engage in a letter-writing campaign seeking U.S. participation in an international network of food reserves.

Along with social concerns, the ALC has continued to exhibit strong interest in evangelism and mission. Beginning in 1977, the ALC joined the LCA in emphasizing evangelical outreach. Congregations were encouraged to study the biblical basis for gospel witness, to strengthen their outreach to unchurched persons, to seek to restore

44

inactive members, and to develop ways to integrate members into the life and mission of the Christian community.

The Lutheran Vespers radio ministry is broadcast under ALC auspices.

The United Mission Appeal so captured the imagination of ALC members that they oversubscribed the appeal—to the extent of $37 million. Appeal funds were used to extend ALC involvement overseas and gave fresh initiative to the planting of new congregations (which in the late 1970s was at about the rate of 30 a year). In the late 1970s the ALC had some 400 persons serving as full-time missionaries in work with young churches in 18 countries. Other ALC lay persons have gone as part-time mission helpers to fields around the world under the World Brotherhood Exchange, an agency started under ALC auspices which later became part of the Lutheran Council in the U.S.A. Other ALC members have traveled to the church's mission fields at their own expense, and nationals have come to this country to visit ALC congregations. A major interchurch consultation bringing 33 leaders from overseas churches was sponsored in July-August 1978 by the ALC Division for World Mission and Inter-Church Cooperation. The leaders spent 10 days in all of the ALC's 18 districts as part of their sharing experience.

The ALC is known for its strong church colleges, and this is perhaps one of its main strengths. The ALC senior colleges are Augsburg, Minneapolis; Augustana, Sioux Falls, S.D.; California Lutheran, Thousand Oaks, Calif.; Capital University, Columbus, Ohio; Concordia, Moorhead, Minn.; Dana, Blair, Neb.; Luther, Decorah, Iowa; Pacific Lutheran University, Tacoma, Wash.; St. Olaf, Northfield, Minn.; Texas Lutheran, Seguin, Tex., and Wartburg, Waverly, Iowa. LCA synods are represented on the boards of and give support to California Lutheran, Pacific Lutheran, and Texas Lutheran, and the ALC has a relationship to the LCA's Carthage College in Kenosha, Wis.

The ALC trains its men and women for the ministry at its seminaries—in St. Paul, Columbus, and Dubuque—and at the LCA seminary in Berkeley, with which it cooperates.

In a preface to a book of essays noting the centennial of Luther Seminary, St. Paul, Dr. Lloyd Svendsbye, Luther's president, cites the flexibility the seminary has had in tolerating and making creative use of differences of outlook and emphasis in doctrinal and hermeneutical problems.

"Luther Seminary," he writes, "has never insisted upon theological or ecclesiastical uniformity. Differences in ways of worship, interpretation of doctrine, or methods of evangelism have produced intense discussions and at times heightened anxieties, but have been contained within a common loyalty to Jesus Christ and the Gospel. They have resulted in diversity but not in division." This perhaps has been the genius of all the ALC seminaries.

The ALC colleges and seminaries, along with the inter-Lutheran campus ministry, benefited from an appeal for $20 million that the ALC conducted in the late 1960s. On the whole, ALC colleges have continued to be healthy, though faced with the same situation threatening other small, private colleges—escalating costs, with student enrollment holding steady or slipping slightly. As with the student population generally, in the late 1970s quietism replaced the fervor of the 1960s.

The ALC and its congregations assist some 200 social service agencies, including more than 125 Lutheran homes for the aging.

Augsburg Publishing House, which the ALC owns and

operates, has become one of the nation's leading church-owned Protestant publishing houses. *The Lutheran Standard*, published by the ALC, reached a circulation of some 540,000 in the late 1970s, as most of the ALC districts adopted an every-member circulation plan. The Augsburg "Good News" curriculum received wide acceptance by ALC congregations.

American Lutheran Church Women has been a vigorous auxiliary of the church, providing funds for a host of projects, including many involving mission.

In the late 1970s special attention was focused in the ALC upon women's role in church and society. By a vote of 560 to 414, the ALC decided at its 1970 convention to admit women to its ministry. The first ALC woman minister, Barbara Andrews, was ordained in late 1973 in a suburban Minneapolis church. By 1978, the ALC had ordained 27 women. Enrollment of women in ALC seminaries expanded rapidly.

A larger role for women in running the church and an end to sexism in the church's worship were urged by women's task forces.

Many ALC pastors and congregations have become involved in the charismatic renewal movement. A statement recognizing the movement was adopted by the ALC at its 1976 convention in Washington, D.C. The ALC has attempted to maintain links with ALC members involved in the movement, learning from them, but at the same time expressing concern over certain aspects of the movement.

Since the ALC began, it has been a member of the World Council of Churches. It has not joined the National Council of Churches, although some of its divisions participate in NCC divisions. A number of ALC districts now participate in state councils of churches or ecumenical associations. Historically, congregations of the ALC and its predecessor bodies were slow to take part in interdenominational services, but spurred by the example of the World Council of Churches and by the Second Vatican Council on the world level, more and more engage in ecumenical worship, mostly on special occasions.

The ALC has been a strong partner in the Lutheran World Federation, with one of its clergymen (Fredrik A. Schiotz) serving as LWF president and two of its pastors (S.C. Michelfelder and Carl Mau) serving as LWF general secretary. Other ALC members have served in other LWF staff positions and on its commissions and committees.

Increasingly, the ALC has been shedding its rural image as members move to urban settings and to the Sunbelt. Population movements also have meant that the ALC is constantly feeding the leadership life of other churches.

*   *   *

A brief description of the four ALC antecedent bodies follows:

A merger in 1930 had formed the old ALC, uniting the Ohio, Buffalo, and Iowa Synods. (The Texas Synod had already become a district of the Iowa Synod.) The Ohio Synod developed out of home missionary work of the Ministerium of Pennsylvania among Ohio Valley settlers in the early 1800s. The Buffalo Synod was organized in 1845 by Prussian Lutherans who fled oppression in their homeland for refusing to participate in the Prussian Union. The Iowa Synod was organized in 1854, an outgrowth of the spiritual interest of Wilhelm Loehe of Bavaria in the spiritual welfare of German immigrants. Constituent synods of the old ALC carried on negotiations with the Missouri Synod from

1917 to 1929 and again from 1934 to 1956 when they were dropped because of the ALC merger plans. Presidents of the old ALC were C.C. Hein, Emanuel Poppen, and Henry F. Schuh. Its headquarters were in Columbus, Ohio.

The ELC was founded in 1917 and was known until 1946 as the Norwegian Lutheran Church in America. The 1917 merger brought together Hauge's Synod, formed in 1876 by pietistic followers of Norwegian revivalist Hans Nielsen Hauge; the Norwegian Synod, formed in 1853 by Lutherans known for strict adherence to Lutheran doctrine and practice; and a middle group known as the United Norwegian Church, formed in 1890 by merger of three churches. (One of the latter churches had the unecumenical name of the "Anti-Missourian Brotherhood.") The first permanent congregations among the Norwegian settlers were organized in northern Illinois and southwestern Wisconsin. The ELC dated its founding to the founding of the Muskego church near Madison, Wis. Presidents of the ELC were H.G. Stub, J.A. Aasgaard, and F.A. Schiotz. Its headquarters were in Minneapolis.

The UELC was known until 1946 as the United Danish Evangelical Lutheran Church, with headquarters in Blair, Neb. It was organized in Minneapolis in 1896 by two synods akin in spirit to the Inner Mission Movement in Denmark—North Church and Blair Church. Its Trinity Theological Seminary at Blair was founded in 1884. It was merged with Wartburg Seminary in Dubuque, Iowa, in 1961. Presidents of the UELC were G.B. Christiansen, N.M. Andreasen, N.C. Carlsen, Hans C. Jersild, and William Larsen. Dr. Carlsen issued the invitation to the merger discussions that led to formation of the ALC.

The LFC was formed in 1897 in Minneapolis and grew out of a spiritual awakening that swept over parts of the

Upper Midwest among Norse Lutherans. Not intended originally as a new denomination, the movement eventually became that and was centered around Augsburg College and Seminary, Minneapolis. The movement emphasized a vital experience of Christian life, democratic church polity, and lay preaching. After the LFC joined the ALC, Augsburg Seminary became a part of Luther Seminary, St. Paul. The four men who served as full-time presidents of the LFC were Endre E. Gynild, Hans J. Urdahl, Thorvald O. Burntvedt and John Stensvaag.

The Wisconsin
Evangelical Lutheran Synod

The Wisconsin Evangelical Lutheran Synod is one of the most conservative of all Lutheran bodies.

In the 1970s it was growing while most other large Lutheran bodies were losing members.

In the 25-year period ending in 1977, it increased its baptized membership from 316,839 to 400,201. During the same period, the number of congregations increased from 837 to 1089.

The Wisconsin Synod didn't start out as a conservative body. It tolerated diverse theological views until it was "straightened out" by the Missouri Synod.

For 90 years the Wisconsin and Missouri Synods were allied in the Evangelical Lutheran Synodical Conference of North America. The two synods exchanged pastors, had intercommunion, and did mission work together. But in 1961 the Wisconsin Synod suspended fellowship with the Missouri Synod, charging that it had departed from its original confessional position and was becoming liberal. Specifically, it objected to growing contacts the Missouri

51

Synod was having with Lutheran bodies not in the conference and with which it was not yet in doctrinal agreement.

In 1963 the Wisconsin Synod withdrew from the Synodical Conference. The Evangelical Lutheran Synod, another conservative body, also withdrew.

As a result, the Synodical Conference was left with two surviving members—the Missouri Synod and the Synod of Evangelical Lutheran Churches (Slovak). The latter two bodies later formed the Lutheran Council in the U.S.A., along with the LCA and the ALC.

The Wisconsin Synod was organized in 1850 at a little church outside of Milwaukee by three missionaries sent from Germany to work among German Lutherans in Wisconsin. For 17 years it received support from "union" (Lutheran and Reformed) mission societies in Germany, but in 1868 ended ties with them and decided to be strictly Lutheran.

In 1892 the Wisconsin Synod formed a federation with two somewhat smaller synods, similar in background—the Minnesota and Michigan Synods. They united in 1917 as the Evangelical Lutheran Joint Synod of Wisconsin and Other States. This name was changed in 1959 to the Wisconsin Evangelical Lutheran Synod.

The Wisconsin Synod, as might be expected, is strongest in Wisconsin. Minnesota and Michigan have the next largest concentration of congregations. The Dakotas, Iowa, Nebraska, Illinois, Arizona, California, Washington, and Colorado come next.

Since 1893 the Wisconsin Synod has been working among the Apache Indians of Arizona. American Mother of the Year for 1967 was the widow of a Wisconsin Synod pastor to the Apaches, Mrs. Minnie Guenther, Whiteriver, Ariz.

The Wisconsin Synod is known for its uncompromising

dedication to orthodox, confessional Lutheranism. It teaches word-for-word verbal inspiration of the Bible, accepts Scripture as "true and without error in everything it says," believes that creation took place in six normal days, and rejects evolution and any attempts to reduce the first chapters of Genesis to a narration of symbolic myths. It also rejects "the attempts to make the historicity of events in Christ's life, such as His virgin birth, His miracles or His bodily resurrection, appear unimportant or even doubtful."

Boy Scout troops are not permitted in Wisconsin Synod congregations because they are thought to have religious elements obscuring the teaching that humanity's salvation is entirely in the hands of God. For similar reasons the synod does not accept members of lodges with religious ritual.

The synod believes in strict separation of church and state. It does not permit its pastors to accept appointments as government chaplains in the armed forces, believing that they would not be able to practice the synod's religious convictions. It has received permission to use civilian chaplains to serve its members on domestic and foreign military bases. One of them spent 18 months in Vietnam.

In line with its views on church and state, the synod has asked its congregations to exercise extreme caution in accepting any government aid for their parochial schools.

As a church body, the synod did not concern itself with the civil rights struggle, the war on poverty, or the war in Vietnam. But it does believe that members, as Christian citizens, are and should be concerned with social issues.

The synod believes that telling the world that in Christ their sins are forgiven "is the church's business" and that this assignment demands all its time and resources.

The Wisconsin Synod says it is not isolationist and is

willing to meet with any church body at any time, any place to discuss doctrine and practice, provided the other body admits the necessity of determining whether agreement or differences in doctrine and practice exist and agrees that differences must be removed before there can be fellowship.

Next to its loyalty to the Scriptures and the Lutheran Confessions, the Wisconsin Synod perhaps most cherishes its educational system. The synod has its seminary in Mequon, Wis., and its colleges and academies in Watertown and Milwaukee, Wis.; New Ulm, Minn.; Saginaw, Mich., and Mobridge, S.D. Synod congregations in 1978 were operating 312 Christian day schools, with a total elementary enrollment of 29,010. In addition, there were 11 area Lutheran high schools.

Because of booming enrollments at the colleges in New Ulm and Watertown, the synod at its 1977 convention took action looking toward relocation of academies it operates on those two campuses. At a special convention in 1978, the synod voted to consolidate the pre-teacher training programs offered at the two academies. For the new site, the synod voted to purchase the 108-acre campus of the former Campion High School at Prairie du Chien, Wis., a Jesuit boarding school which ceased operation in 1975. Another proposal being studied calls for relocation of the academy in Mobridge to the Southwest, possibly Arizona or California, to serve an area where the synod has experienced rapid growth in recent years.

The synod's Commission on Higher Education projected that by the year 2000 the synod would need 82 to 125 pastors and 282 new teachers annually to serve the synod's growing membership.

The Wisconsin Synod observed its 125th anniversary in

1975 with a thankoffering called "Grace 125." The goal was $2.8 million, but more than $3.5 million was raised. Proceeds were used for capital funds at the synod's Michigan preparatory school, world mission fields, and church extension. Earlier, the 1966-68 "Missio Dei" ("Mission of God") appeal raised $5.5 million for synod educational facilities. The goal was $4 million.

In 1978, the Wisconsin Synod accepted an invitation from the Lutheran Church–Missouri Synod to take part in informal talks between the two synods "with the understanding that the talks will be conducted outside the framework of fellowship."

The Wisconsin Synod's Commission on Inter-Church Relations, which sent observers to the 1977 Dallas convention of the Missouri Synod, reported favorably on conservative trends at the convention. The commission referred specifically to Missouri's declaration of "fellowship in protest" with the American Lutheran Church, to its deferring of action on the Inter-Lutheran Book of Worship, which has been criticized by Missouri Synod conservatives, and to its rejection of the historical-critical method of biblical interpretation.

At its 1977 convention in New Ulm, the Wisconsin Synod reelected the Rev. Oscar J. Naumann to his 13th successive two-year term as president. Until 1953 the synod presidency was a part-time position and President Naumann also served a congregation in St. Paul. Beginning in 1969 he served the synod full-time from its national headquarters in Milwaukee.

Since the 1917 merger, other Wisconsin Synod presidents have been the Rev. G.E. Bergemann (1917-33) and the Rev. John Brenner (1933-53).

The Association of
Evangelical Lutheran Churches

THE newest of U.S. Lutheran denominations hopes to
have a short existence.

The Association of Evangelical Lutheran Churches was
organized in late 1976 as a new home for those "moderate"
congregations and pastors in the Lutheran Church–Missouri
Synod unhappy with the larger denomination's administra-
tive and theological direction.

At its second convention in 1976, the AELC approved a
proposal intended to facilitate its disappearance. By almost
unanimous voice vote, the convention approved "A Call
for Lutheran Union."

The AELC invited "all Lutheran bodies in North
America to join us in making a formal commitment to
organic union in a design in which Lutheran life and
mission may be consolidated at all levels."

The call envisioned a fall 1979 consultation to "establish
an implementation process in which the people of the
church at the congregational and judicatory (regional unit)
levels will have full participation."

While the Lutheran Church–Missouri Synod and the Wisconsin Evangelical Lutheran Synod were to be invited to participate in the union consultations with the other Lutheran bodies, their acceptances were considered unlikely.

Thus the AELC invitation appeared primarily addressed to the Lutheran Church in America and the American Lutheran Church. Judging by comments made by their presidents at the 1978 AELC convention, the LCA appeared the more enthusiastic about the call to union. LCA President Robert Marshall told the AELC convention that the LCA would receive its call "with a great round of applause and eagerly join you in a process to effect that union."

But ALC President David W. Preus pointed out that the ALC had recently completed years of reorganization efforts and said it was not time for another round of intensive concern with organizational matters. While affirming that the future of U.S. Lutherans is together, he said the ALC would prefer a process of "evolving development" and urged the AELC to accept an invitation to join the ALC-LCA committee on church cooperation which is ironing out structural differences between the bodies.

The AELC has its roots in the movement of "confession and protest" which 800 "moderate" LCMS pastors and lay persons organized in Chicago in August 1973 as Evangelical Lutherans in Mission (ELIM). The movement was a reaction to decisions of the LCMS, particularly the LCMS convention charges of heresy against the faculty of Concordia Seminary, St. Louis. ELIM organizers said the movement would seek to change the LCMS from within.

When most of the faculty and students at Concordia left the former seminary early in 1974, that breakaway seminary became the central focus of ELIM resources. The ELIM missions agency, called Partners in Mission, was started to hook up mission projects with donors in a personal way.

As Christ Seminary–Seminex and Partners in Mission began seeking separate funding, ELIM's budget dropped from $1.6 million to $200,000. The main projects ELIM had left were communications and its newspaper, *Missouri in Perspective,* which once had a circulation of 155,000 but which had fallen to 46,000 in 1978.

ELIM never had an official membership, but counted as its supporters those who contributed to it. The list of contributors once totaled about 8000. Increasingly, ELIM came under attack from LCMS leaders who accused it of being divisive. District presidents, synod staff, and faculty members of synod colleges and seminaries who supported it were threatened with dismissal.

As the split in the LCMS grew, some congregations and pastors decided a protest movement was not enough and that the time had come to organize new synods. They formed five: the English Synod (concentrated in the Upper Midwest from Minneapolis to Cleveland and including the Chicago and Detroit areas), the Great River Synod (which stretched south to Louisiana), the East Coast Synod, the Southwest Synod, and the Pacific Coast Synod.

These five synods organized the AELC in 1976. The AELC's first president was the Rev. William Kohn, a Milwaukee pastor and a former LCMS missions official. For a while, some of the congregations and pastors in the AELC continued to hold membership in the LCMS, but they were ordered by the 1977 LCMS convention to make a choice between the two bodies. By the time of its second convention in 1978, the AELC had 245 congregations, with some 110,000 baptized members in its ranks.

By 1978 the AELC had become a member of several cooperative groups—the Lutheran World Federation, Lutheran World Ministries, the Lutheran Council in the U.S.A., and Lutheran World Relief.

Only time would tell whether the AELC would become the bridge bringing together the ALC and LCA. President Kohn, defending the AELC "call to union," said the call may seem to be "hasty action."

But, he noted, "we did not intend to form a church body which would be ongoing. We talked of an approximate 10-year existence. It could well take that long to achieve whatever might be adopted."

Other Lutheran Groups

THE FIVE largest Lutheran bodies have a combined membership of more than 8.5 million members. In addition, there are (or have been) about 10 other Lutheran bodies, much smaller in size, whose combined U.S. membership is less than 100,000.

The Evangelical Lutheran Synod, organized in 1918 as the Norwegian Synod of the American Evangelical Lutheran Church, was formed by a minority group declining to enter the 1917 union that formed the Norwegian Lutheran Church of America, later known as the Evangelical Lutheran Church and now merged into the ALC. The cause of the separation was a dispute over the doctrinal issues of election and grace.

The ELS, as it is known, for some years trained its pastors and teachers at the colleges and seminaries of the Missouri and Wisconsin Synods. It now has its own seminary and junior college at Mankato, Minn., where the denominational headquarters are located. The ELS continued in fellowship with the Wisconsin Synod after breaking fellowship with the Missouri Synod and leaving the Synodical Conference. In 1978 it accepted an invitation for doctrinal talks with the Missouri Synod that could lead to renewed ties.

The ELS has about 20,000 members in 106 congregations.

The Association of Free Lutheran Congregations was formed in 1962 by congregations of the former Lutheran Free Church declining to enter the merger that created the ALC. It also has accepted churches from other bodies and some that were independent. A 1977 report indicated it had 127 congregations with 14,000 members. The association stresses autonomy of the local congregation and has a pietistic and evangelistic emphasis. It operates a seminary and Bible school in Plymouth, Minn., a Minneapolis suburb, where it also has its headquarters.

The Church of the Lutheran Brethren of America, organized in 1900 in Milwaukee by Lutherans of Norwegian background, differs from other Lutheran churches in that it accepts as members only those who profess a personal experience of salvation. It is "low church" and without liturgy. Communion is received in the pew. There are no altars, and the pastors do not wear gowns or robes. Headquarters are in Fergus Falls, Minn., where the synod also operates a seminary, a Bible school, and a high school. The denomination has some 8600 baptized members in 90 congregations.

The Apostolic Lutheran Church of America originated with Finnish immigrants in and around Calumet, Mich., in the middle of the 19th century. It was organized in 1872 under the name of Solomon Korteniemi Lutheran Society. In 1929 it was incorporated as the Finnish Apostolic Lutheran Church of America. "Finnish" was dropped from the name in 1962. The synod requires a scriptural Christian experience as a condition for voting membership in spiritual matters and puts strong emphasis on confession of sins, absolution, and regeneration. Those who fall into sin known to others are required to make public confession. The synod has some 9300 members in 64 congregations.

Two other small Lutheran bodies were formed by Wisconsin Synod dissidents. The Protestant Conference (Lutheran) was organized in 1927 by members seeking to correct the "spirit of self-righteousness and self-sufficiency" in the synod. It has some 1400 members. The Church of the Lutheran Confession was formed by Wisconsin Synod members who felt the synod was too slow in cutting ties with the Missouri Synod. It has nearly 10,000 members.

There also were two small splinter groups formed by Missouri Synod dissidents who were protesting "liberal" trends in that denomination. A split in one of them resulted in still another group.

The Orthodox Lutheran Conference was organized in 1951 at Okabena, Minn., by 10 pastors who had left the LCMS, charging liberalism. When it dissolved in 1962, it had four pastors, six congregations, and 450 baptized members. Most of the pastors and congregations joined the Wisconsin Synod.

The Concordia Lutheran Conference was organized in 1959 by pastors who left the Orthodox Lutheran Conference, charging it with false doctrine. For a while, both groups called themselves the Orthodox Lutheran Conference, but in the summer of 1960 the group that left reorganized under the name Concordia Lutheran Conference. It reported in 1978 that it had five pastors and congregations, with 450 members.

The Federation for Authentic Lutheranism was organized in 1971 in Libertyville, Ill., by about a dozen pastors who had withdrawn from the LCMS charging it with liberalism. It dissolved in 1975. Its 12 congregations (with 4000 members) either joined the Wisconsin Synod or the Evangelical Lutheran Synod or remained independent.

A tiny group facing extinction is the Eielsen Synod (Evangelical Lutheran Church in America), which was organized among Norwegians in 1846 and is named for Elling Eielsen, a preacher active in the revival movement inspired by Hans Nielsen Hauge of Norway. It has insisted upon proof of conversion as a prerequisite for membership. Its last reported membership was considerably below 500.

The former Synod of Evangelical Lutheran Churches, a largely Slovak body, has become a nongeographical district of the Lutheran Church–Missouri Synod. It was to have been absorbed into LCMS geographical districts by 1977, but the date for completion of the merger has been indefinitely postponed. It has some 20,000 members.

The Evangelical Lutheran Church of Canada is the former Canada district of the American Lutheran Church, which became an independent church in 1967. It has 82,000 members and has been actively working to promote union with Canadian units of the Lutheran Church in America and the Lutheran Church–Missouri Synod.